Every Breath You Take

How to Breathe Your Way to a Mindful Life

Rose Elliot

WATKINS

Sharing Wisdom Since
1893

This edition first published in the UK and USA 2016 by

Watkins, an imprint of Watkins Media Limited

19 Cecil Court

London WC2N 4EZ

enquiries@watkinspublishing.com

1 3 5 7 9 10 8 6 4 2

Designer: Gail Jones

Printed and bound in Bosnia & Herzegovina

A CIP record for this book is available from the British Library

ISBN: 978-178028-981-6

www.watkinspublishing.com

Contents

Prologue

'We are all born with the perfect tool for mindfulness. One that is with us all the time, that we can connect with wherever we are, whatever we are going through, and that will never let us down: it's our breath.'

ROSE ELLIOT, *I MET A MONK*

Introduction
How It All Began

Like many people, I had heard about mindfulness. I knew that it meant paying attention, opening our awareness to what is happening in the present moment, and accepting it without judging or trying to control it.

I knew also that practising mindfulness has been shown to have many benefits – more peace, energy, self-confidence, less stress, relief from depression and anxiety, fewer aches and pains – and I wanted to experience some of those for myself.

However, much as I tried, I struggled with the practice. I found it dreary, dull and boring – all that 'notice-what-you're-doing-while-you-clean-your-teeth' – I just couldn't get to grips with it at all.

I know that the experts say that when done correctly mindfulness is never boring, but it was for me. I kept trying, but I just couldn't sustain it.

Then, when I was on the point of giving up altogether, I met a monk – an experience that I have described in my

book, *I Met A Monk* – and he quietly suggested that it
is helpful to link mindfulness practice to breathing.

This really helped. In fact it helped so much that I
decided to do some research on mindfulness. What I
discovered nearly took my breath away, if I can say that.
It has certainly changed my life.

I found that, in its original form, mindfulness was in
fact actually based on our breathing; the breath was an
intrinsic part of it.

Mindfulness and breathing go together, and when you
practise mindfulness with the breath, what might have
been a dull, boring and mechanical practice suddenly
comes alive. It is like putting petrol in your tank or the
wind beneath your sails: mindfulness becomes a really
enjoyable experience that just seems to flow.

Practising mindfulness using your breath as the
starting point and the focus, not only opens your
awareness to the present moment, which is what
mindfulness is all about, but it can also naturally put you
in touch with more peace, joy, strength – and, dare I say it,
wisdom – which you may never have known you had. If
you wish – and once you get started, you probably will – it

can naturally lead into a meditation practice, with all the many health and wellbeing benefits that this is proven to bring. It is truly life changing.

Once you know how to breathe mindfully, you can do it anywhere, any time, any place; it's like flicking on an instant 'inner peace' switch. And it certainly is not boring!

So join me now, as we go back 2,500 years to the night when the first teaching on mindfulness was given: when mindfulness began...

The moon was full, the crowd were still...

It was the end of the rainy season in India. Several hundred people were gathered and waited expectantly.

A tall, slim, dark-haired man was sitting cross-legged in front of them. He looked around the gathering thoughtfully and then, after a pause, he spoke...

He spoke words that would help ordinary people, from all walks of life; the people who listened to him that night; and the millions more who would hear them in the future, as they echoed down the centuries to our present time: how to do mindfulness breathing and so find inner peace, strength and healing, whatever your situation or walk of life.

The world has changed beyond all recognition since then, but human beings and the problems we face haven't; the teaching is as fresh and helpful today as it was all those centuries ago.

So this book is based on the instructions the Buddha gave then, in the form of simple breathing exercises. These run like a golden thread throughout the book, showing how we can develop mindfulness of the breath and use it in every aspect of life: our body, feelings, emotions, mind and spirit.

In practice, all these areas of life overlap and interweave, affecting each other, so as you become mindful of one, the others benefit as well, bringing an increasing sense of balance and harmony to your life.

Practising mindfulness breathing for a few minutes each day as explained, will allow this beautiful, ancient practice and wisdom to heal your life from the inside out, bringing increasing peace, freedom and joy.

If you can breathe, you can be mindful, and if you can be mindful, you can heal and transform your life.

Welcome!

As I have explained, it is to the Buddha that we owe mindfulness, but that does not mean you have to 'be a Buddhist' (whatever that may mean), or indeed of any religion at all to practise it. The breath is universal, as is spirit, so we can all benefit.

I love the simple, down-to-earth teaching that the Buddha gave, but I do not label myself 'Buddhist', or anything else, for that matter. For me, just being human is enough. I resonate very much with the words of the French idealist philosopher Pierre Teilhard de Chardin, who said, 'We are not human beings having a spiritual experience. We are spiritual beings having a human experience.'

Anyway, whatever your own background or personal beliefs, whether you have practised mindfulness before or are completely new to it, I hope you will find this book helpful.

Mindfulness breathing brings calmness, peace and an inner strength and joy that gently permeate your whole life.

What the Buddha said

This book is based on the actual words that the Buddha spoke that night, called the *Anapanasati Sutta*, in which he brought the teaching of mindfulness to the world. Like all of the Buddha's teaching, it was given in the spoken language of Northern India at the time, Pali, learnt through repetition, and handed down over two or three centuries until it could be written down. As the teaching has spread to the north, south, east and west there have been many translations of the Sutta, but the overall teaching has remained consistent. This book is based on a version devised by the author and Zen Buddhist monk Thich Nhat Hanh, and I am giving it here for reference, but we will consider it gradually, line by line, in 16 breathing exercises, as we go through the book. Thich Nhat Hanh said that when he first came upon this teaching he felt like the happiest person in the world, and I have to say I know exactly what he means. I do hope as you read this book and practise the breathing, you will know too.

The teaching consists of 16 ways of being mindful, starting with the simple mindfulness breath upon which it is all based, and ending with nirvana: as the wise Buddhist monk and teacher Ajahn Fuang said, 'The breath can take you all the way to nirvana…'

Try it for yourself, and see.

Anapanasati Sutta
by Thich Nhat Hanh

1. Breathing in, I know I am breathing in.
    Breathing out, I know I am breathing out.
2. Breathing in, I know I am breathing in. a long
    breath or a short breath. Breathing out, I know
    I am breathing out a long breath or a short
    breath.
3. Breathing in, I am aware of the whole body.
    Breathing out, I am aware of the whole body.
4. Breathing in, I calm the whole body. Breathing
    out, I calm the whole body.
5. Breathing in, I feel happy. Breathing out,
    I feel happy.
6. Breathing in, I feel bliss. Breathing out,
    I feel bliss.
7. Breathing in, I am aware of the feeling that is
    present now. Breathing out, I am aware of the
    feeling that is present now.

8. Breathing in, I calm the feeling that is present now. Breathing out, I calm the feeling that is present now.
9. Breathing in, I am aware of the mind. Breathing out, I am aware of the mind.
10. Breathing in, I make my mind happy. Breathing out, I make my mind happy.
11. Breathing in, I concentrate my mind. Breathing out, I concentrate my mind.
12. Breathing in, I liberate my mind. Breathing out, I liberate my mind.
13. Breathing in, I observe the impermanence of life. Breathing out, I observe the impermanence life.
14. Breathing in, I observe the disappearance of desire. Breathing out, I observe the disappearance of desire.
15. Breathing in, I observe cessation. Breathing out, I observe cessation.
16. Breathing in, I observe letting go. Breathing out, I observe letting go.[1]

Chapter 1

How To Breathe Mindfully

'When mindfulness of breathing is developed and cultivated it is of great benefit.'

THE BUDDHA

So what is mindfulness breathing?

Being mindful of your breath simply means observing and opening your awareness to your breath: to your breathing in and your breathing out, without controlling or judging it in any way: letting it be. That's it – it's that easy!

Once you've become practised at breathing mindfully, you will find that it becomes natural for you and at any time you choose to do so. Simply combining your breathing with whatever you are doing will help you transition into a mindful state of being. The practice will become a part of you and your daily life.

However, when you're learning mindfulness breathing it's best to do it sitting comfortably in a quiet place with your eyes closed. This is so that you can focus on your breathing without any distractions.

You will very soon get the feel for it – a minute or two of practice here and there – literally, we're talking 1–2 minutes of practice two to three times a day – and soon mindfulness breathing becomes second nature – like swimming or riding a bicycle.

Then you will find that you can take a mindfulness breath any place, any time, without closing your eyes.

It's as if you just 'click into' mindfulness mode and then you can expand your mindfulness to anything that you wish, or to the world in general, with the gentle breathing going on at the same time, gently supporting and sustaining you. It's a wonderful process.

So let's get started...

Breathing Exercise 1

'Breathing in, I know I am breathing in. Breathing out, I know I am breathing out.'

Find a quiet place and sit down comfortably with your spine straight

Close your eyes and through closed eyelids focus your attention on the tip of your nose or, as the Buddha said, 'in front of the face' – at the tip of the nose, looking slightly downward (through closed eyes). It's almost as though you are wearing a diving mask and looking slightly downward through it, but with your eyes shut...

Then, as you focus your attention on the tip of your nose (or in front of your face), you notice the breath going in, and coming out again.

You don't have to follow the passage of the breath right inside your body and into your lungs, just notice it going in and coming out through your nose.

Continue to breathe, noticing the in-breath and

the out-breath at the tip of your nose – or wherever you feel it. It's where *you* actually feel it that matters, not where you think you should be feeling it; open yourself to the experience as it feels for you.

Once you have done this for a few breaths, add the following words:

As you breathe in, you think to yourself, 'Breathing in I know I am breathing in.'

And as you breathe out, you think, 'Breathing out, I know I am breathing out.'

Saying those words to yourself helps to keep your awareness on your breath so that your mind doesn't stray on to other things – but if your mind does wander, just bring it gently back to your breath, and to the words.

Open your awareness to what you are experiencing, as you breathe. Do not change your breathing at all; just be aware of it.

Repeat this exercise gently two or three times, and see how you get on. Keep doing it from time to time until you get used to it.

Once you've got the hang of this, you can shorten the words to 'in/out' if you prefer by saying 'in' as you breathe in, and 'out' as you breathe out.

Sitting quietly... we focus on one mindful breath after another. We feel the peace and the strength that this brings... in this moment, all is well.

My experience: **Learning the breathing**

At first the mindfulness breathing felt rather unnatural: coordinating my mind with my inhalations and exhalations felt strange. But I found the more I managed to stop thinking about the process and really opened myself to what I was actually feeling, the easier it became. I was aware of the air at the tip of my nose, going up inside my nose, cool and refreshing, then much lower down, in the middle of my chest, and finally coming out of my nostrils again, often with surprising force.

Practising

Once you become familiar with the exercise, there's no need to keep saying 'in/out'. You can simply open your awareness to the full experience of feeling the air enter and leave your nostrils. But if you find that saying 'in/out' helps you to keep your mind free from intrusive thoughts, by all means continue. In this way 'in/out' can be used like a mantra to accompany your breathing and keep part of your mind busy so that your main attention remains focused on your breath. Or you might like to say the words for the first two or three breaths to get you started, and then let them fall away as you get absorbed in your breathing.

Notice the quality of your breath. You may find that it changes and becomes slower and deeper; there is no need to judge it at all; just notice it, be aware of it, without making any inner comment on it: that's being mindful.

When you feel comfortable breathing like this –
focusing (through closed eyes) on the tip of your nose as
described – you can move on to the next breathing exercise.

Again, this exercise helps you to focus on your breath
and also to open your awareness to the quality of it:
whether it's short, or long...

Breathing Exercise 2

*'Breathing in, I know I am breathing in a long breath
or a short breath. Breathing out, I know I am breathing
out a long breath or a short breath.'*

That's rather a long statement for a simple idea!
It doesn't matter at all whether your breaths are
'short' or 'long'; you are not trying to judge or trying
to change them.

What you are saying, as you breathe in and
breathe out, is simply a reminder to you to notice
the nature of the breath without changing it at all.

So allow your breaths to be as they are – basically,

you're saying if you breathe in short, you breathe in short; if you breathe in long, you breathe in long, so be it, that's the way it is... short or long, let it be... but you are being aware of it, that is the main thing.

Again, if you wish, you can abbreviate the words to 'short or long' as you breathe in, and 'short or long' as you breathe out. Saying the words helps keep your chattering mind occupied, freeing you to open your awareness to your breath, but once you can focus on your breathing for the whole breath without getting distracted by your thoughts, you do not need to keep saying the words.

It is important, though, to remember that we are not at any point controlling or judging our breath.

We are simply aiming to feel and experience each breath as it actually is. It may be long or short, deep or shallow, smooth or jerky... it is as it is. But as we open our awareness to our breathing it will naturally become slower and deeper.

Tips for breathing

1 While you are practising, and getting the feel of mindfulness breathing, keep your eyes closed: this will help you to open your awareness to your breathing.

2 Remember to focus on the tip of your nose (or as if you are looking very slightly down (but not lowering your head at all) through a diving face mask), and to notice your breath as it goes into your nostrils, and as it comes out.

3 Keep your awareness on your breaths all the way through without interruption, if possible — this will come with practice.

4 Open yourself to the whole experience. Be completely 'with' the breath for those few seconds.

5 If a thought comes, don't try to suppress it, or feel irritated with yourself: simply take yourself back to your breathing.

6 Don't try consciously to change the length of your

breaths, or anything else; just really notice the
feeling of your breath.

7 Enjoy your breathing!

How to practise

With each of the 16 breathing exercises, start with two
or three breaths, perhaps doing this two or three times
during the day, or whenever you think about it – or you
can do it more often if you wish: the more you do it, the
easier and more natural it will become.

Every breath you take mindfully is helpful; three
mindfulness breaths every hour could have a noticeable
effect; and if you can gradually build up the time, the
benefits will only increase... It all helps.

Harvard-affiliated researchers at Massachusetts
General Hospital found that practising mindfulness for
10 minutes a day is enough to bring positive results in
about 6–8 weeks... but take your time to build up to this:
there's no rush.[2]

If you set an alarm to remind you every hour, and
then breathe mindfully for 1 minute, and do this

throughout the day – not that difficult, actually – that would be your 10 minutes done!

You just need to persevere a little at the beginning until the mindfulness breathing feels natural, then, the more you do it, the better it gets, and the better it gets, the more you will actually want to do it.

Taking a mindfulness breath whenever you think about it will bring you almost instant peace – and you can simply build on this, allowing it to become a part of your life, like breathing itself. That's a mindfulness approach: just opening yourself up to the practice...

You breathe all the time, so why not make every breath a mindfulness breath?

My experience: **Practising the breathing**

Practising mindfulness breathing for just a few seconds at a time really helped me when I first started. I found I came to really enjoy it and was able to build the time up gradually. Once I could maintain mindfulness for 1 minute I set the alarm on my watch to go off and now I love this reminder: I say to myself, if I do nothing else, I'm being mindful for a few seconds every hour – and they build up over the course of the day.

Finding peace within

After a while you may find that you almost become a part of your 'in' and your 'out' breaths.

At first this may just be for the merest second, but as you practise regularly, you will find taking the breaths becomes easier, and it may begin to feel as though you have a clear space within you as you breathe. As you continue, your awareness of this clear space will last longer.

It can begin to feel like a safe place where you can go to whenever you feel afraid, upset or worried.

You can return to it at any time, while you are at work or at play, no matter what else is going on.

This place of peace is always there for you, and the more you practise mindfulness breathing, the stronger it will get.

Just take a mindfulness breath to get you there; feel the air going in and out of your nostrils; feel the peace this brings.

Just breathe...

Feel the air entering your nose... and passing out again.

Feel the peace this brings, the way it calms you.

Breathe again, in, out...

Feel the peace, the way the breath connects you with your own inner strength, no matter what is going on around you.

Breathe...

Widening your practice

Once you've learnt how to be mindful of your breath and practised it so that it begins to feel natural, you can expand your mindfulness to embrace other areas of your life.

I think of mindfulness as being rather like the lens on a camera: you start by focusing it just on your breath, then you can 'open the lens' – gently expand your mindfulness to embrace your body, your feelings, what you are currently doing or the distant skyline – you can 'point your mindfulness lens' at whatever you choose to, being fully aware of whatever you are focusing on, and with your steady breathing continuing in the background all the time.

So, you:

- Make the intention to be mindful.
- Decide where you are going to 'point your mindfulness lens'.
- Decide whether you are going to open your lens – your awareness – wide, perhaps to the whole of your environment – or to focus it on one particular thing. You are always in charge and can make these choices,

and change them at any time, such as when you're doing a body scan (see page 59) – in which you concentrate on each part of your body in turn – and you move your 'mindfulness lens' over your body, taking in different parts, from the whole body to your toes, even your toenails… but wherever you are pointing your lens, and whatever focus you are using, you are opening your awareness to what is happening for you in the present moment, without any judgement or comment. It's as if you are seeing it and experiencing it for the very first time, through newborn eyes and complete innocence.

Keep it simple

Just breathe; follow your breath. Feel the peace.

- Try taking another mindfulness breath, and then another…
- See if you can do it for a minute. I tell you, a minute will probably never have seemed as long as it does when you first do this!
- Gradually build up the time that you can hold your awareness of this clear space, and the peace that it

brings. Open yourself to it.

- Keep doing it throughout the day, whenever you think about it.
- Or do it on the hour, every hour; do it more often if you wish: every 5, 10, 15, 20 minutes, whenever you need to feel stronger, more focused, more at peace; and always when you feel worried, fearful, or in any way troubled.

My experience: **Practising mindfulness**

I love practising mindfulness in this way; just doing it, and feeling the effect it has on me, and on my life generally. Because life does change when you start mindfulness breathing. It affects you from the inside out. You begin to feel calmer, stronger, more focused and more positive about life; and as you change, so the way people behave to you changes, and the world around you changes. It does begin to feel like a kind of magic.

Breathing goes on at the very centre of our being, involving the function that keeps us alive — our intake of oxygen. So when we practise mindfulness of the breath, we are uniting our mind with this life-giving activity, making it very powerful.

Chapter 2
Heal Your Body

'I have a body but I am more than my body. I have feelings but I am more than my feelings. I have a mind but I am more than my mind. I am a centre of pure awareness, love and will.'

ROBERTO ASSAGIOLI

We need our body; we could not live our life without it, and yet many of us have mixed feelings about it. We may tolerate our body because we have no choice, but we may criticize its look, its shape or its condition; it may cause us mental, physical or emotional pain. We may take out our frustration and anger by overeating, starving, self-harming or extreme exercise; we may feel alienated from our body.

As we learn to be mindful of our body, our attitude toward it changes.

We begin to take notice of how it is feeling; listen to the signals it is giving us, start caring for it better, perhaps notice little discomforts and inconveniences we can correct to make it feel more at ease: more comfortable shoes and clothes; an office chair that is the right height; nurturing food and drinks; exercise that helps it to be strong, flexible and free. We become reconciled to our body – get to love it, even; allow it to heal naturally, and we feel the benefit.

And it all starts with this simple and relaxing breathing exercise: Allow yourself a few minutes of peace to practise.

Breathing Exercise 3

'Breathing in, I am aware of the whole body. Breathing out, I am aware of the whole body.'
You can do this exercise in any position, sitting in a relaxed way with your spine straight and your feet on the floor or, for more relaxation, lying on your back with your head on a pillow and your legs straight or with knees bent. Whatever position you choose, make sure you are comfortable.

In this exercise, instead of saying 'my body' it helps to create a little space by saying 'the body', as if we are gently observing it; but if this feels unnatural to you, it's also fine to say 'my body'.

Take a mindful breath to settle yourself.

So, breathe in, and say to yourself, 'Breathing in, I am aware of the whole body.'

And, as you breathe out, say, 'Breathing out, I am aware of the whole body.'

Open your awareness to what you are feeling: the air going in through your nostrils (or wherever you first feel it), down into your body and then out again through your nose.

Just notice what you can feel. You will become more sensitive to the feeling of the breath as your mindfulness breathing practice deepens.

Continue for a few breaths, feel the body relax and surrender to the breath, the life-giving oxygen entering the blood stream, reaching every part of the body, every atom, then leaving the body replenished, healed and strengthened.

If random thoughts come to you, just bring your attention gently back to your breathing as soon as you notice; take another breath, feel the air going into you, soothing you, embracing your whole body.

For these few seconds, your mind and body are one – and you are at peace – wholly in the present moment: your mind and your body united 'in the now'.

Enjoy this feeling then gently open your eyes, move, stretch a little and return to your life.

Remember the peace you have just experienced is only a mindfulness breath away. You can return to it often, at any time, any place.

The body of the breath

In the breathing exercise we have just done, when we refer to 'the whole body' – 'breathing in, I experience the whole body, breathing out, I experience the whole body' – we are talking about the physical body, but we are also referring to the 'body' of the breath – that is, all the air, the inhalation, as we breathe it in and out.

This is quite subtle but, as you practise and your mindfulness increases, you may become increasingly aware of the feeling of the form or 'shape' of the breath, (or 'body'), as it enters and leaves your physical body, and both of them as separate entities.

My experience: **The body of the breath**

The idea of the breath as a 'body' seemed quite unusual to me at first, but I gave it a try, and was surprised how I was able to become aware of 'the body' of the breath. Now when I do the Whole Body Breathing (Breathing Exercise 3, see page 43), it feels

as if my body is a container for the breath, and I
am being mindful of them both. I like that feeling.
It brings to mind some words by the psychiatrist and
pioneer of humanist and transpersonal psychology,
Roberto Assagioli, who I quoted at the start of this
chapter (see page 42).

Whether or not you are aware of the 'body of the breath'
at first, as you practise breathing mindfully your
awareness of your physical body will naturally increase.
You may notice when you become tense and perhaps
clench your fists or your jaw, hunch your shoulders or
hold your breath. You can respond by using Breathing
Exercise 3: letting go of the tension, and taking a
mindfulness breath. Or you can soothe your body with
the following breathing exercise, the fourth exercise that
the Buddha gave. Or you can use both exercises; think
of them as interchangeable and to be used whenever
you feel uncomfortable in your body or want to nurture
peace and love in your mind.

Breathing Exercise 4

'Breathing in, I calm the whole body. Breathing out,
I calm the whole body.'

As before, you can practise this in any position, but when you are first learning it, it's helpful to make sure you are feeling comfortable, and have a few minutes of peace in a safe place where you can close your eyes.

Breathe in, saying to yourself, 'Calming the whole body, I breathe in.'

Breathe out, saying, 'Calming the whole body, I breathe out.'

Be aware of the air as it goes into your body, through your nostrils – or wherever you can first feel it – filling you, and then leaving.

Feel the calm, the peace, this brings.

Again, you can return to this at any time, night or day, whenever you want to reconnect with this peace – it is always there for you. And the more you check in to it, the easier and more natural the process becomes, and the more aware you will become of the sense of peace and strength that it brings.

You can vary the wording, saying whatever feels right to you at the time, such as 'healing the body', 'soothing the body', or 'embracing the body'; make the practice your own: enjoy it.

When you're mindful of your breath, it can become like your best friend, a friend who is always with you, always wise, always has your best interests at heart – a friend who can work miracles, as those who practise increasingly find, and you will too.

Practising

Having a breathing practice may at first seem a little strange – being aware of your breath, following it as it enters, fills and leaves your body – but gradually it begins to feel more natural, and the sense of peace and inner strength that it brings gradually builds. Try:

- Taking a mindfulness breath on the hour throughout the day.
- Three breaths – or breathing mindfully for 1 minute, which will most likely be more than three breaths (I often find I take five breaths in a minute) – three or four times a day.
- Breathing mindfully as often as you can, whenever you think of it.

This will become more natural over a period of a few weeks, and you'll certainly feel the benefit.

As your practice continues so your breathing naturally become deeper, slower. You begin to experience the peace and harmony mindfulness breathing can bring.

Living mindfully

It's helpful to build mindfulness breathing into your regular daily routine so you can practise naturally, as you go about your daily life. You may find, as I did, that there is much joy and satisfaction to be had when you do any task mindfully, as you open your awareness first to your breathing and then expand it to embrace what you are doing – experiencing the sounds, sights, feelings, scents, as if for the first time.

So how do you do this?

- Breathe…
- Do one thing at a time.
- Keep your mind on what you are doing, really experience it, without judgement or criticism.
- When your mind wanders, bring it back to the present moment and what you are doing: pause briefly and take a mindfulness breath; close your eyes, feel the air as it enters your nose, follow it going in, and out again.
- Feel the peace and strength this brings – then get back to your task while you keep your awareness of your breathing going on in the background.

Eating mindfully

This practice is something to do when you are on your own, and have the time…

Take a breath; notice how your body is feeling.

Open your awareness to the food that you are about to eat: the colour, the aroma…

Take a mindfulness breath, as you learnt to do in Breathing Exercise 1 (see page 24), and breathe between mouthfuls...

Feel the quality of the food in your mouth; the texture, the temperature, the flavour, the consistency.

Chew, chew, chew – until the food turns to liquid in your mouth, if you can: 40–100 times – very meditative! As I said, probably not something to practise when you're in company...

Breathe...

Feel the peace, feel the joy...

Peace throughout the day

You can use the irritations of daily life as reminders to take a mindfulness breath – and this way you'll certainly get plenty of practice! For instance, such reminders might be:

· Being held up by traffic or a red light when you are driving.

· Waiting for the kettle to boil or for a bus or a train

that's late – waiting for almost anything.

- Lining up at the bank or at the grocery store checkout, or anywhere, for that matter.
- When someone is being really irritating: how great to know you have your own inner source of peace so they can't bother you.
- When you're feeling sad or angry: we'll look at this in more detail in the next chapter (see page 92).

Your mindfulness breathing will carry you through all these times, and more, and as I hope you are finding, the more you practise it, the better it gets...

Walking meditation

One of the most pleasant ways of practising mindfulness breathing is by doing a 'walking meditation'.

Walking meditation simply means you set out with the intention of walking mindfully, for a period of time, or a certain distance. You can practise walking mindfully anywhere, any time.

Start by taking a few mindful breaths to compose yourself: feel the breath filling your body, and open your awareness to the legs, ankles and feet, particularly the soles of the feet.

Feel the feet planted on the solid ground beneath you, supporting you, and then just notice them moving forward, and walk, and breathe...

Open your awareness to your walking, and to what you are experiencing in your body; your breathing; and any sensations you feel, such as the breeze on your face.

Try not to get distracted either by internal thoughts, or by what you see or hear. Keep bringing your awareness back to what you are directly experiencing moment by moment; to your in-breath and your out-breath; you may feel you have become one with your breathing.

When random thoughts come to you, as soon as you realize, simply take a mindfulness breath and open your awareness again to your experience of walking.

You can walk fast or slowly. You can walk in rhythm with your breathing, taking one step on your in-breath and the next with your out-breath, or you can walk more quickly, with two or three steps to each inhalation and exhalation; allow your body to find a comfortable rhythm, so that you can open your awareness to your breathing and what you are experiencing.

Keeping focused in a walking meditation

If you are in a restless mood and your mind keeps wandering:

- Try to see if you can keep up some steady counting, perhaps up to ten, and then start again from one, or whatever feels comfortable for you.
- Or you can say a simple mantra to keep the thought-filled part of your mind busy so that the awareness part

of it can continue to open to your breathing and the action of walking.

- The much-loved Buddhist teacher, Thich Nhat Hanh suggests saying 'I have arrived' as you breathe in and take a step, and 'I am home' as you breathe out and take the next step. Or if you want to walk at a faster pace, you can take two or three steps with each in-breath and out-breath and perhaps say, 'I've arrived, arrived, arrived' and 'I'm home, home, home.'[1] I like the feeling of safety and groundedness this brings.

Find your own comfortable rhythm as you enjoy the feeling of your in-breath and your out-breath, and the movement of your body, and you will find that walking mindfully is a joy.

Becoming mindful of our breath enables us to open our awareness to the whole of our body, accepting it, healing it.

My experience: **Mindful walking**

When I am walking mindfully I often think of something else that Thich Nhat Hanh said. He likened taking a step to placing a seal on the ground, with mindfulness as the ink.[1] So instead of printing worry, depression, haste or anger with our steps, as we might do when rushing around normally, when we step mindfully, we can print a seal of peace upon the earth. I love that thought. What if everyone started printing their seal upon the earth with the ink of mindfulness? Could we change the world that way, d'you think?

Body scan

When you can spare 10–15 minutes, a body scan is a lovely form of 'body mindfulness' you can do – it's well worth taking the time. You can do it sitting or lying down, with your eyes closed or open. It's most relaxing when done lying down, with your eyes closed; make sure you are comfortable and won't be disturbed.

- Take a mindfulness breath or two to anchor and settle you. Get a sense of the position of your body; how it is feeling – whether there is any tension or pain.
- Notice also how you are feeling – just notice, as though you are looking down on yourself. Are you calm, tense, restless – or perhaps there is no feeling. We are not judging, just observing.
- Be aware of your mind. Is it active, or passive... restless, or peaceful? Again, simply notice, there's no judgement.
- Take another breath; notice where you start

feeling it, and follow it in, and out of your body...
just notice.

- Now we will begin our scan of the body, starting
  with the feet and working upward, noticing how
  each part of the body is feeling in turn – whether
  it's warm or cold, tense or relaxed, heavy or light,
  prickly or itchy – whatever it is feeling – or if you
  can't feel it, then notice that. We are just noticing
  what we are experiencing, and we are not judging.
- So begin by noticing your feet: any sensations in
  the soles of the feet, the toes, the tops of the feet, the
  ankles. Whatever you feel, or don't feel, let it be.
- Now move up the legs, bringing your attention to
  the front and the back of the calves and shins, the
  knees and up the thighs to the hips.
- Move your attention to your lower abdomen,
  the front and the back, with awareness of the
  digestive organs and emotions that you may
  feel stored in this area of the body... and then up
  through the waist and into the chest... being aware

of the life-giving heart and lungs, as you feel your breath going in and out...

- Then up to your shoulders, aware of any tension you are holding here... and down from your shoulders to the backs and fronts of your arms, and your hands and fingers...

- And then up to the neck, being aware of any tension here; and from the neck to the chin and the jaw; the back of the neck, the ears and the scalp; the face, the cheeks, the eyes, the forehead, and up to the crown of the head.

- Now take a nice deep mindfulness breath, letting go of any tension, with awareness of the head and face and arms and hands, chest, abdomen, hips and legs and feet... breathing in and noticing how the whole body expands; breathing out and noticing how the whole body contracts, getting a sense of the body as a whole, and gently moving, stretching, coming back, and perhaps feeling a sense of gratitude for having had this experience.

Embrace each part of your body with mindfulness and love, like a mother caring for her child... feel the gentle healing power this brings.

My experience: **Mindfulness pain relief**

Mindfulness has an unexpected benefit that I have discovered from personal experience: pain relief. I have found that if I am experiencing some ache or discomfort, or have to go through some uncomfortable medical procedure, taking some gentle mindfulness breaths can really help, and on one or two occasions in my life mindfulness breathing has enabled me to cope with really intense pain, such as giving birth – it felt as though I was above my body, looking down on it, feeling-it-but-not-feeling-it; 'riding the pain'.

This is not to say I'm not grateful for – and use – painkillers when I need them, but there are many occasions – having an injection, a mammogram, or a visit to the dentist – when taking a mindfulness breath really helps.

The healing breath

Taking a mindfulness breath helps you find healing.

As you focus on your breathing you become more peaceful.

You can let go of fears and worries, aches and pains – physical, mental and emotional – as the breath lifts you out of the pain and takes you to a place of peace and healing deep within.

My experience: **A mindfulness day**

I like to have a minute or two of mindfulness breathing when I wake up, while I'm still in bed, if I can; then the same at lunch time, but not in bed, of course; and again sometime in the evening; and throughout the day whenever I think of it – certainly if I feel upset, or worried. I take a mindfulness walk when I can fit it in, maybe walking to the shops... and I love to take a few mindfulness breaths just before I fall asleep – I always seem to sleep well and wake up feeling peaceful and happy when I do that. If that sounds like a lot of mindfulness, well, I suppose it is, but only consisting of a minute or two at a time. All I can say is it works for me, and the more you do it, the more you'll want to do it!

Can you be mindful all the time?

We have to use our minds to plan, to make decisions, to deal with our lives. But we can do these things with an attitude of mindfulness. That's where mindfulness breathing is so practical, because we are breathing all the time, so any breath can be a mindfulness breath, if we make it one, and connecting us with our own inner peace and strength. You can take a mindfulness breath no matter what else you are doing, without disturbing your thinking process; it's like a steady heartbeat of peace and strength going on in the background of your life, whatever you are doing.

Your mindfulness breaths may seem like little oases of peace in a busy day. The more you do them, the more natural it will seem, the more peace and strength you will feel and carry through your day from hour to hour... this alone can change your life; it has mine.

Chapter 3
Calm Your Feelings

'The past is already gone. The future is not here. There is only one moment for you to live. That is the present time.'

THE BUDDHA

So we have experienced opening our awareness to our breath, and widened this to include our physical body, and now we come to our feelings.

So what exactly do we mean by feelings and how can we be mindful of them?

When the Buddha spoke about being mindful of the feelings, he meant both bodily sensations, such as warmth, hunger or physical pain, and feelings such as happiness, sadness, boredom and so on.

But unless we are being rocked by some big emotion, many of us find it quite difficult to identify what we are feeling emotionally; we tend to blank off from it, yet the feelings are often there beneath the surface causing a kind of underlying lack of ease, worry or sadness that we may carry as tension or even pain in our physical body.

Becoming mindful of our feelings, instead of consciously or unconsciously suppressing them, enables us to understand what is going on, and find peace and healing – and more energy and happiness too.

And we can do that now. As the body and emotions are so closely linked, noticing how our body is feeling is a good way of opening the door to awareness of the state of our emotions too. We can do it with this quick check:

Quick body check

This is a quick scan that you can do in less than 5 minutes, sitting at your desk, or wherever you happen to be.

Pause whatever you are doing, and if it is safe to do so, close your eyes.

Take a mindfulness breath: feel the air entering and leaving your nostrils, grounding, calming and centring you.

Then continue to breathe mindfully for a few breaths, gently, opening your awareness to the state of your body from top to toe.

So, noticing tensions and feelings in the body, and

letting them go, open your awareness to:

• **The crown of your head and over your face:** are your eyes tight, your jaws clenched, any other areas of tension? Release the tension; let it go.

• **Your neck, is it tense?** Are your shoulders hunched? Shrug your shoulders a few times to loosen them, let the tension go.

• **Your upper arms, and down the arms to your hands** – maybe shake your lower arms and hands. Relax your palms and fingers.

• **Next, your chest, abdomen and lower back down to the base of the spine.**

• **Then move down to your thighs, knees, shins and ankles, feet and toes, tensing and relaxing them in turn, letting the tension go.**

• **Then take a mindfulness 'body breath' or two (see page 43):** feeling as if you are breathing life-giving air into your whole body, stretch a little and open your eyes, and come back to your life refreshed.

If you find it difficult to 'feel your feelings', it can be helpful to 'check in' to yourself at regular intervals during the day. Don't judge what you find; simply notice. This will help you develop awareness of your feelings.

My experience: **Quick body check**

When I first did the quick body check, I was surprised to notice that I wasn't feeling much; I just felt neutral, a kind of blankness — although that in itself is a valid awareness, and it was true for me at that moment. I think if I had done it when I was actually feeling upset about something, it would have been different. It can be helpful to 'check in' with your feelings from time to time, especially if you find you tend to be a bit out of touch with them.

When you're happy and you know it...

According to the Buddha, the other thing we can do to open our awareness to our feelings is to notice when we are happy!

That's rather clever when you think about it, because we all want to feel happy, so it's much easier and more pleasant practising becoming more aware of our feelings by noticing when we are happy.

But let's be clear: eventually we need to become more aware of *all* our feelings, but if we're shut off from them at the moment, it's easier to open the door by looking for the happy ones first.

We can do this in two ways:

1. Practising the following breathing exercise in which we notice the happiness within us, which in turn helps us to activate reserves of joy that we have deeper inside.

2. Looking for ways to create more happiness by the way we live our life.

We'll start with the breathing, but before we do this, there is something I need to explain: it's about the power of intention, and how this fits in with mindfulness.

The power of intention

We know that mindfulness means opening our awareness to something without judging or controlling it. So how, you might ask, does *making the intention* to focus on feelings of happiness, rather than on whatever feelings may be present, fit in with mindfulness?

'Intention' is a power that we have within us, like energy or inner will.

It's our power of intention that we are using when we direct our mindfulness 'lens' on to whatever we choose, and decide whether to make our mindfulness focus wide or narrow (see page 35). In the same way, our power of intention enables us to be selective in the feelings that we are going to open ourselves to – and rather than opening our awareness to whatever feelings we have, at this moment, in this exercise, we are using our power of intention to open ourselves to the feelings of happiness that may be present – or that we can awaken.

So now let's try the next exercise – the happiness breath.

Breathing Exercise 5

'Breathing in, I feel happy. Breathing out, I feel happy.'
   To do this exercise, you prepare in the usual way
– find a place where it's safe to close your eyes and
where you can be quiet for a few minutes – then
you take a mindfulness breath and open yourself to
feelings of happiness.

   In doing this, you are simply using your intention
to open yourself, at this moment, to feelings of
happiness: it's a choice. You're programming your
inner lens to detect happiness, if you like; to focus on
that, rather than any other feeling at this moment.

   So, as you breathe in, you say, 'Breathing in, I feel
happy.'

   And as you breathe out, you say, 'Breathing out,
I feel happy.'

   Enjoy the feeling of the air going in through your
nose and down into your body; the release and
relaxation as you let it out...

Don't worry if you do not feel anything much, just focus on the feeling of the cool air passing through your nostrils and going down into your body, then out again...

You could think of something in your life that makes you feel happy now, or has made you happy in the past and use that to help you evoke the feeling of happiness.

Simply concentrating on the pleasure of the feeling of the breath going in and out and the inner peace and calm this brings could also help you to build up your inner happiness pool.

The breath nurturing you, soothing you...

The peace that this brings... the happiness of that feeling, of knowing that in this moment, all is well...

Do this exercise a few times – just a few breaths at odd moments – when you have the time, and you will find that the inner joy will build.

My experience: **The happiness breath**

I enjoyed this exercise and was surprised how much happiness I felt. I also realized how much of what we experience is what we are looking for, as if we set our inner compass to it and so get drawn toward it, or certainly notice it more. It seems that if you make the intention to notice happiness, your happiness receptors, as it were, begin to get more sensitive to detecting it – or maybe you give out a joyful vibration that attracts it: perhaps it's a bit of both.

Ways to feel happy

Along with practising the 'happiness breath', we can make the intention to bring more happiness into our daily life, and the two things – the breath, and the practical 'sourcing' of happiness – work together, reinforcing each other.

It is easier to be happy, positive and optimistic if you were brought up to view life in that way, but if that was not the case for you, don't be put off. Anyone can learn to be happy, at any age. In fact, research has shown that there are certain simple things you can do to help you experience more happiness, and thus become more in touch with your feelings.[3-5] These include:

- Being in the present moment.
- Accepting things as they are.
- Being mindful of the simple pleasures of life.
- Being kind.
- Being grateful.

We will take them in turn, and see if we can really get that 'happiness muscle' working!

Being in the present moment

The breathing practices we have done so far, the walking meditation and the body scan, all help us to be mindful, to be aware of the present moment, or, as they say, to 'be in the now'.

When you are being mindful of the present moment, to everything that is happening now, it means letting go of all preconceived ideas and opinions, and all fears about the future, because in the present moment there is no past, and no future. You are accepting everything exactly as it is now: 'it is as it is'.

It is a bit of an adjustment to get your head around this, but once you do – and the more you practise, the easier it becomes – it's such a boost to the level of happiness you feel. In fact, if I had to write the secret of happiness down in just three words, it would be this: BE PRESENT NOW.

In the English language the word for this moment now – the present – is the same as the word that means 'a gift'.

Accepting things as they are

This is such an important key to happiness, and of course all part of 'being in the now'. When we can accept things as they are, it takes away so much of the aggro, the emotional charge. Things are as they are – and that's *all*

they are! We make them into something more by
our thoughts and the descriptions we attach to them.

We bring pain and suffering on ourselves by
projecting on to things meaning they don't have.

Try to notice when you do this – and how much more
peaceful you feel when you just accept things as they are,
including yourself. That is being mindful, being aware of
things as they are at this moment, and accepting them,
and letting them be, without judging them.

When you criticize, grumble, complain, or think
harmful thoughts about someone or something, you
actually hurt yourself.

When we make judgements we give
things meaning they don't have,
because, when we're mindful, they
just 'are'; in the present moment,
'it is as it is', and that is all.

My experience: **The pain of judgement**

Since I've been practising mindfulness I have noticed something strange. I've found that when I make a judgement or criticism, it actually hurts me physically! It feels like an ache or a little stabbing pain in my heart. I was very surprised when I started noticing this, but now I am used to it. It does make me think twice, though, about making judgements and criticisms, let alone saying anything unkind! And so I have become much more accepting, and I do wonder whether this is something other people experience, although I have never heard it mentioned.

I find it helpful to remember the words of Ajahn Chah, the wonderful monk who brought Theravada Buddhism to the West. He used to say, 'It's good enough', and I often apply this to things I am doing, or the way things are. I say, 'It's good enough' or 'I'm good enough' – and feel the tension go. And when people were *gossiping idly, and generally making statements that were not wise or mindful, he would say, 'Is that so?' and I find this a useful comment too.*

Being mindful of the simple pleasures of life

Make the intention to be mindful of – and allow yourself – the simple pleasures of life, the things *you* enjoy. For instance:

- A hot shower, a steaming cup of coffee, the feeling of the sunshine on your face, the smell of toast.
- Seeing the green grass or a beautiful tree.
- Hearing the song of the birds or the snatch of a haunting melody or the sound of a loved one's voice.
- When the work is done, allowing yourself to do things you really love doing: a crossword, crochet or knitting with beautiful coloured yarns, drawing and painting, a walk or a run... small things that bring you pleasure... make time for them.

The more of these simple pleasures you find, the more you'll notice your happiness increase: a small practical example of the positive effect of mindfulness...

One of the secrets of a happy life is continuous small treats.

IRIS MURDOCH

Being kind

Being kind brings happiness. This has been proved scientifically. In one study, the level of serotonin (our happiness-inducing hormone) was found to rise when someone had done a kind act. Interestingly, it was also found to rise in the person who had been the recipient of the kindness, and also in those who had witnessed the kindness being done, who then went onto give themselves![6]

In Buddhism, 'loving kindness' is called *metta* and the practice is one of its cornerstones. You can't have too much loving kindness; and it starts with your attitude to yourself. So:

- Be kind and gentle with yourself.
- Deep down, we all have the same feelings; we want to be loved, happy, respected, secure; so treat other people as you would like to be treated – why wouldn't you?

  – and watch the kindness and happiness spread, like

ripples on a pool. The more kindness you put out, the more you'll get back. Try it and see: you'll be amazed how much kindness comes to you. We could change the world that way, along with our mindful walking I described earlier!

If you want to be happy, start by being kind and loving with yourself, especially when you're sad, depressed, or afraid.

Metta practice

The Buddha had a formal way of practising loving kindness with some words you can say. It may feel strange at first, and as though nothing is happening, but somewhere deep down it is resonating, and you will feel the benefits. The words are:

'May I be safe. May I be happy. May I be well and at ease.'

They are a wonderful mantra to have: you could use them when you are doing a walking meditation (see page 54), or any time.

You may think it is selfish to say 'may *I* be happy', but you have to get yourself right before you can help others – rather like having to put on your own oxygen mask in an aircraft before you help others fit theirs.

When you feel comfortable about saying the metta words for yourself, you then extend them to other people. You think of someone, and say, 'May you be safe. May you be happy. May you be well and at ease.'

In the Buddhist tradition, you do this with someone you love; someone who you respect and who has helped you – who the Buddha called 'a patron'; someone you feel neutral about, an acquaintance, maybe; and someone you hate, dislike or have issues with – that's the testing one! But it really works; you have to persist for a while, perhaps doing it every day for a few weeks, but it's worth it for the beautiful feeling of peace and love it will bring you.

'My religion is loving kindness. Without loving kindness the human race cannot survive.'

HIS HOLINESS, THE 14TH DALAI LAMA

Be grateful

Bringing to mind all the things in life that you're grateful for makes you feel happier, too: you can really experience the uplifting effect of this. You could start a 'gratitude practice' – regularly listing a number of things you feel grateful for in your life. Some people do this every evening; cultivating what that wise teacher, the late Wayne Dyer, called 'an attitude of gratitude', is a very helpful and positive thing to do.

Try a bit of 'gratitude practice' next time you are feeling sad. Whilst acknowledging, and certainly not glossing over, the sadness, turn your mind to the things in your life that you are grateful for. I often do this and I can vouch for the healing it brings. Even on the dullest, saddest days, it's possible to think of something to be grateful for, even if it's only the calming effect of the feeling of the breath going in through your nose and the release of letting it go; the firmness of the ground beneath your feet, the smile of a stranger, the sound of a bird. Once you start practising gratitude, you'll be surprised how the habit builds up, and, as with many things, like attracts like: the more you notice things to be grateful for, the more of them you'll find.

You might also like to write some of the things you are grateful for on a postcard – perhaps using different coloured inks to make the words stand out – and use it as an aide memoire to lift your spirits whenever you're in need of a little joy.

Bliss

Maybe after some 'happiness practice' you might feel ready to attempt the Buddha's next breathing exercise, which takes happiness a step further: this time we're looking for bliss, no less!

But don't let's split hairs at this point about the difference between happiness and bliss (or different words for happiness and bliss, such as joy and rapture, which are used in some translations of the Buddha's breathing exercises). We can just settle for 'happiness' at this point, or 'joy' if you like, although as the practice goes on, maybe it will be appropriate to say 'bliss'. It is certainly possible to reach a state of bliss through mindfulness breathing.

'My general formula for my students is "follow your bliss". Find where it is, and don't be afraid to follow it.'

JOSEPH CAMPBELL

Breathing Exercise 6

'Breathing in, I feel bliss. Breathing out, I feel bliss.'
Take a mindfulness breath and open yourself to
feelings of bliss – joy – happiness...

As before, you are using your intention (see page
75) to open yourself at this moment, to evoke these
feelings...

So, as you breathe in, say, 'Breathing in, I feel bliss.'

And as you breathe out, you say, 'Breathing out, I
feel bliss.'

This will become easier – don't worry if you can't
feel much at the moment. You can come back to
it later – or make a point of doing it at some time
when you are truly experiencing such feelings.

In any case, enjoy the feeling of the air going into
your nose and down into your body; the release and
relaxation as you let it out... feel the peace. That is
the beginning of 'bliss'... it will come.

Being mindful of how we are feeling right now

Once we've become more aware of our feelings through specifically noticing our feelings of happiness, we can gently widen this practice and open ourselves to exactly how we are feeling at any moment

When we do this, we are not directing our 'mindfulness lens' specifically toward feelings of happiness; now we are breathing in, and simply opening ourselves to the awareness of our feelings.

There is no need to be afraid of this process; you are opening yourself to your feelings through the protection of your breath.

If at any time you feel afraid or worried, simply switch your awareness completely on to the feeling of the breath itself, protecting and comforting you – keeping you safe.

In this exercise it is helpful to say 'the feelings' rather than 'my feelings' because it gives a little space between them and us.

Breathing Exercise 7

'Breathing in, I am aware of the feeling that is present now. Breathing out, I am aware of the feeling that is present now.'

Close your eyes, take a mindfulness breath, feeling the air going in through your nostrils, into your body, and out of your nostrils, and at the same time, notice the feelings that are present.

As you breathe in and out say,' Breathing in, I am aware of the feelings present now. Breathing out, I am aware of the feelings present now.'

Really open yourself to the feelings, whether they are pleasant or not. Remember, you are safe, protected by your breath.

You are just 'being aware' of the feelings, observing, being, just as you did when you were mindful of your body.

You are not judging your feelings; you are not trying to fix them; you are simply observing, allowing.

Keep breathing; keep watching the feelings, almost as if you are sitting above your head, looking down on yourself, on your feelings, and allowing them to be.

Keep gently breathing, and saying to yourself, 'Breathing out, I am aware of the feeling that is present now.'

When you have had enough, take another mindfulness breath or two, perhaps feeling the breath go right through your body, as we did in the body breath (see Breathing Exercise 3, page 43), healing, nurturing and protecting you.

'Every breath we take, every step we make, can be filled with peace, joy and serenity.'

THICH NHAT HANH

Feeling the feelings

When you do this as an exercise it is quite possible
that you won't feel much. But it is still helpful to do it,
because it gets you used to tuning in to your feelings, so
when an upsetting one does come along, you can take a
mindfulness breath and notice it, rather than blocking it
off. Remember:

- Breathe, and allow yourself to open to your feelings.
  You are safe with the breath. Breathe and be with the
  pain, the fear, the sadness or the worry. Breathe, and let
  it be there, but continue to take gentle breaths and feel
  the peace and comfort that they bring.
- Don't try to change your feelings, or wish them to be
  different: just accept them exactly as they are – without
  judging them as being 'good' or 'bad' – just that they are
  feelings. Keep gently breathing.
- Don't embroider them with 'what ifs?' or 'if onlys' or
  with feeling sorry for yourself, or by blaming yourself
  or anyone else for the situation.
- Say, 'It is as it is' and allow it to be.
- Don't try to hurry it, but know that it will change,

because everything does; and accepting it rather than fighting it will bring you peace now.

Like the caterpillar in its chrysalis turning into a butterfly, change will happen. Nurture and protect your chrysalis – and watch the beautiful butterfly emerge when it's ready.

Once you've been through this process, or seen people who are close to you do so, you have more confidence that this quiet acceptance works. You can't hurry the process of healing, but you can ease things a little:

· Be in the present moment: breathe.
· Accept, even embrace, the pain; knowing it will pass – everything passes.

Staying with difficult feelings

Remember, in any mindfulness practice that you do, *to stay with the feeling*: open yourself to it and accept it exactly as it is.

This is not difficult to do with feelings of pleasure – although sometimes they can get mixed up with feelings of guilt or fear that the pleasure will end – but it can be challenging when the feelings are unpleasant.

It seems counterintuitive to allow painful emotions such as grief, jealousy, fear or anger, to be – or even encourage them – but that is the way to heal them. It's no good banging on the floorboards in the hope that those below will quieten down, as it's likely to make them louder!

There is a story the Buddha told to his followers that graphically illustrates the power of acceptance in dealing with difficult feelings. The Buddha told it specifically regarding anger (I told a version of this story in *I Met a Monk*, but I wanted to include here again – albeit with a slightly different retelling – because it is so graphic, and relevant to all negative states). It goes like this.

'A sickly and decrepit-looking demon took his seat on the throne of Sakka, the leader of the gods. This angered the rest of the gods, who shouted at the demon, and as they did so, the demon grew bigger and more and more handsome: the angrier they became, the bigger and more handsome the demon became, because he fed on anger.

When Sakka heard what was happening, he did not join in the anger. He dropped to his knees in front of the demon saying, "Sir, I am your obedient servant, Sakka, the leader of the gods." He did this three times, and each time the demon shrank and became more sickly looking, until he finally disappeared.'

That's what happens to the anger or other negative emotions we may be feeling when we allow them to be, give them space inside us and some loving kindness.

My experience: **One breath at a time...**

When you're going through a sad or worrying time, it's natural to think of the hours, days, and even years stretching ahead, and wonder, How can I ever go on like this? I caught myself thinking that the other day, and then I suddenly remembered: when we're 'in the now', there is only this moment, this breath; all we have to do is to be mindful of this one breath. Feel the peace and comfort of that – and then take another breath. Peace – and even joy – is only a breath away.

Let us now close this section with the Buddha's breathing exercise in which we use the breath to calm and heal us. We are not denying our feelings, we are not trying to change them; we are accepting them exactly as they are, while we open our awareness to the calming quality of our breath, like putting our arms around a loved one in distress.

Breathing Exercise 8

'Breathing in, I calm the feeling that is present now. Breathing out, I calm the feeling that is present now.'

So close your eyes, take a mindfulness breath, feeling the air going in through your nostrils, into your body, and out of your nose.

Breathe in, say, 'Breathing in, I calm the feelings I am experiencing now.' Breathe out, say, 'Breathing out, I calm the feelings I am experiencing now.'

Allow yourself to feel the feelings; let them be there.

Open your awareness to the breath going in, and the breath going out; only focus on this: breath in, breath out...

Let the breath take its course, don't control it in any way; just notice it.

Let your in-breath and your out-breath fill your mind... that is being mindful of your breath...

Keep noticing your in-breath, your out-breath... feel the breath soothing you... comforting you...

nurturing you. Feel the peace this brings.

Now surrender the issue that is concerning you to this inner peace, to your mindfulness: let the problem go.

Keep breathing, noticing your in-breath and your out-breath...

When the worry or the feeling comes back into your mind and troubles you, repeat the process, noticing and feeling your in-breath and your out-breath... letting your breath fill your mind.

Keep gently repeating this process whenever the worry or the feeling comes back, until eventually it fades away. That's the healing power of mindfulness.

When you have a problem, be mindful, then surrender the issue to your mindfulness self; you will find that things will work out. You may unexpectedly meet someone, see something, get an inspiration; a new direction may come to you out of the blue. Trust your process, trust the healing power of mindfulness.

The power of acceptance and surrender

We have looked at and practised being mindful of our feelings. We have seen how being mindful of our feelings enables us to be aware of how they come and go, to observe them – just as we do our breath – without judging them or identifying with them.

We are beginning to experience how being aware of our breath soothes us; how following it takes us to a place of peace, safety and strength within; and the more we do it, the easier and more natural this becomes...

Mindfulness puts us in touch with a deeper, more 'authentic' part of us, and with our own unique inner power, the power that knows what is right for us, guides and looks after us.

Chapter 4

Soothe Your Mind

'*Calm mind brings inner strength and self-confidence, so that's very important for good health.*'

HIS HOLINESS, THE 14TH DALAI LAMA

We've practised being mindful of our breath, and then widened our awareness to our physical body, and to our feelings. Now we come to mindfulness of the mind – so how can the mind be mindful of itself? That's a good question!

The fact is, the mind is multifaceted – a 'multitasker'. There's the everyday chattering part, full of our moment-to-moment thoughts – 'what shall we have for lunch?', 'Goodness, the traffic outside is noisy today', 'I must pay that bill' and so on... It picks up on our feelings, as well as our chattering thoughts, so it can be a real jumble. No wonder the Buddha described it as 'monkey mind' (or sometimes even as 'drunken monkey mind') – because it jumps around like a monkey (perhaps a bit woozy because of eating too many sweet fruits), swinging from branch to branch of a tree.

There's also a deeper part of the mind that we call 'the subconscious' where thoughts are stored. These may be associated with emotional pain or ordeals that we have experienced or are going through, and they sometimes surface, though we mostly try to keep them hidden away.

And then there is our 'mindfulness mind'. When we use this it feels as if we are getting into an observation space above our head where we can watch what is going on in our mind, and our feelings too. This is the part of our mind we use when we practise mindfulness breathing, and it feels as though there is a part of you that is above you, watching your breath, noticing your feelings and your thoughts. We open our awareness to our thoughts and feelings, or are 'mindful of our mind'.

How it works

It goes like this. You know you've got something on your mind, a problem that's nagging away – or even a situation that's upsetting and you just can't get it out of your mind.

Perhaps you're feeling disturbed about an issue; maybe you're feeling sad or angry or frightened or worried, or a mixture; or maybe there's a feeling that you can't even identify – you just know things aren't right.

Becoming aware of suffering

In order to become aware, first of all, we have to accept that we are suffering. If we ignore the suffering, or tell ourselves it's not there, we are simply blocking it off, burying it in that subconscious part of our mind where it's hard to get to and ready to create further and deeper problems in the future.

But now we are admitting it to ourselves. We are viewing it with our mindfulness mind, as if we are above our mind and looking down into it, viewing the chattering part of our mind, observing. So, just like the body breathing we did, instead of saying to ourselves, 'I am suffering', we can say '*there is* suffering', because it is the 'observer' part of us that is speaking, and acknowledging that something is going on that is causing us pain of some kind.

So we keep noticing, and saying, 'There is suffering.' We stop denying it, closing the door on it, trying to forget, pretending it's not there.

So we admit it: 'There is suffering.' We give it space inside us, in our heart or in our mind, wherever we are feeling it. We make room for it. We open our awareness to it, accept it as it is without making comments or judgements, and allow it to be.

Does that sound familiar? It's exactly the same process as we have been doing regarding our breathing, our body, and our feelings: that's mindfulness!

Let it be

Simply acknowledging what is on our mind and allowing it to be there is the vital first step to finding peace.

When we've done that we do what we always do when we're being mindful of anything – *we let it be*.

We're not judging or analysing it in any way and we are not allowing ourselves to follow our thoughts and get distracted by them – though as we know by now, random thoughts, from our 'monkey mind', do creep in, and when we notice them we simply take another mindfulness breath, and continue with our mindfulness.

When we accept and allow the state of our mind and

our feelings (there's usually a mixture of both, because as you've no doubt already noticed, body, mind and feelings all overlap) and let them be exactly as they are, something interesting happens.

Just as in the story of the king of the gods and the demon (see page 98), they begin to change of their own accord; they subside, and eventually go.

Like any natural process, you can't rush this, though you will begin to see little encouraging signs that the pressure is lessening.

During this process, while the pain and suffering are still around, taking a mindfulness breath of peace when they trouble you will help.

You have to free yourself – and you can. You have the power within you. Trust yourself, trust this tried and tested wisdom.

Here is a simple breathing exercise that will help.

Breathing Exercise 9

'Breathing in, I am aware of the mind. Breathing out, I am aware of the mind.'

Get comfortable with your spine straight. Gently close your eyes and notice your breathing.

Take one or two breaths to prepare, then, as you breathe, say, 'Breathing in, I am aware of the mind; breathing out, I am aware of the mind.'

Take one or two mindfulness breaths as you repeat the words. Then allow yourself to get a sense of what is going on in your mind, as you did before with your body (see page 43).

How does your mind feel? Is it restless? Active? Confused? Damped down? Worried? Wanting something? Annoyed? Or perhaps a mixture?

Whatever is going on in your mind, let it be, without judgement.

Notice, accept, allow it to be.

Breathe...

After a breath or two – several breaths, or several minutes – when you have had enough, take another breath, gently come back to normal consciousness, and open your eyes.

Learning to be mindful of (or becoming mindful of) your own thoughts and feelings is one of the most empowering things you can ever do.

Let it go

When we use our mindfulness to observe our chattering, worrying, suffering, mental states and allow them space to be, they no longer push us around. We know when they are there, but it's as if there is some breathing space between them, and us; we let them be, and then they subside.

And as they go, we begin to feel free from suffering – calm and clear and free from wanting, or hating, or fearing, or indecision and confusion, whatever we were feeling.

As the clouds of suffering and drifting or even thundery thoughts gradually move away, we begin to see clear sky behind them and even glimpse the moon, a beautiful symbol of the mindfulness mind that it is always there for us behind the clouds.

'"Clear mind" is like the full moon in the sky. Sometimes clouds come and cover it, but the moon is always behind them. Clouds go away then the moon shines brightly, so don't worry about "clear mind": it is always there. When thinking comes, behind it is clear mind. When thinking goes, there is only clear mind. Thinking comes and goes, comes and goes. You must not be attached to the coming and the going.'

SEUNG SAHN

There are three simple steps to using mindfulness to ease our state of mind:

1. Accept the worry, the mental suffering, just as it is without judgement, criticism or comment.
2. Let it be.
3. Let it go – which will follow naturally: keep breathing mindfully, which will bring peace and help the process.

If you have tried it, I hope you will have discovered for yourself how well it works. If you haven't yet done so, I suggest you try it next time you have some small problem on your mind, a little decision to make, or a tiny, nagging worry. It's good practice for when you might have to use it for a bigger issue, and will build up your confidence.

My experience: **Letting go of pain**

When I first tried this process I couldn't believe that it would work, but I began being mindful of what was troubling me, and letting it be, not really expecting anything to come of it, but thinking I had nothing to lose... So I was amazed when I started to notice that the nagging, painful thoughts were subsiding… then after a while I forgot about doing the process, and I realized that this was because I wasn't feeling the pain anymore!

Getting to the root of the problem

Once we are familiar with the process, there is more we can do. We can use our mindfulness practice to help us understand a bit more what is going on inside our head, and so free us from repeating the same old cycle of worry. The process follows a familiar pattern: observe, accept and let be, let go.

1. Observe

Remembering we're noticing, not making judgements, not trying to 'get rid of', we open our awareness to the suffering we are feeling, and see if we can identify it further: we are not judging it in any moral way at all: we are just finding out more about it.

The Buddha said that all suffering could be explained by the presence of one (or more) of three feelings: greed, hatred and delusion. So, staying with the suffering that is in your mind (and feelings), allow yourself to really *feel* what it's all about.

Is it greed? An 'I must have', 'I really want', I'm craving for, clinging to, lusting after... Or hatred? A pushing away, an 'I don't want', 'I really hate...' Or delusion? An 'I don't know what I want'; 'I can't choose, I'm going round in circles'; 'I just don't know what to do for the best'.

Or maybe it's a combination of more than one of them.

2. Accept and let be

Let's be clear about this, the Buddha also said these feelings are part of being human and there's no shame attached. But, the important thing is to acknowledge them, and allow them to be there, rather than denying them, because then you can shine your mindfulness light on them, and once you do that, you are in control, no longer at their beck and call, and they are in retreat, disappearing, gone, gone, gone, like the demon, in the story I told earlier (see page 98).

3. Let go

And though the situation may not seem to have changed,

once you've realized what is happening inside you, the very recognition takes the emotional charge away. You can observe it without trying to change it – 'Ah yes, that's greed/hatred/delusion: I can let it go, and find peace,' and as you do so, you will feel it change, and, eventually, evaporate.

The suffering will change and it will pass. Reminding yourself of that whilst not trying to push it away will help you to stay with it until it does.

What about anger – and lack of forgiveness?

When we can't get what we want, or when we fear that we may not be able to do, or when someone does something that harms us, we may get angry. And then what do we do?

We breathe and we allow ourselves to feel the anger or the hurt inside us without getting caught up in it. We watch it as if it were a bonfire and, like a bonfire, as we watch it, and allow it to be, we notice the flames gradually dying down.

Often there is a lot of hurt associated with anger and we can ease the pain of it by doing our best to love ourselves; love brings healing to any situation.

The *metta* practice, described on page 87, is an age-old way of healing hurt feelings, anger, lack of forgiveness and bitterness, or whatever is making your heart feel hard and closed. You don't have to believe it works, just *do* it. Just 5 minutes every day, is that too much to ask for a heart that's free, at peace and full of joy?

You can't have too much metta,
and you can't have too much love.

Forgive yourself

When you slip up, when you fail to reach your own high standards, forgive yourself.

What good does criticizing yourself do? It's simply holding on to something that happened in the past. Let it go.

Breathe and let your breath, now, wash over you, heal you, bring you into the peace and joy of the present moment

Let the past go

Holding on to pain and hurt is the opposite of mindfulness because it involves clinging on to the past.

Breathe, and be in the present moment; release yourself from the grip of the past.

Breathe again; feel the peace inside you.

Feel that tight stone in your heart dissolve so you feel light and free and open to the joy and the love of the present moment.

Freeing yourself from suffering

Use the following four-step process to let go when you notice you're experiencing one of the 'three poisons', as the Buddha called them: greed, hatred or delusion, or possibly a mixture of more than one

1. Get into your 'observer space' in your head.
2. Identify the feeling that is driving your suffering: is it greed? Hatred? Or delusion?
3. If you think it's 'fear', or 'worry', or 'anger', reflect on the feeling that is behind that – and it will be one of the three 'poisons', as the Buddha called them: greed, hatred or delusion, or possibly a mixture of more than one.
4. Once you've identified it, be with the feeling; *really feel the feeling*, allow it to be there.

And watch it start to go... it will

The peace of 'letting be'

The more you allow things to be just as they are, the more you become aware of the peace and strength in this, and in an extraordinary way, you find that the answers to worries and problems just seem to come. It's almost as if the energy of surrender and of letting the worries go, ushers in the solution.

This has happened to me so many times that now I've really come to expect it – the more I surrender any problem or worry I may have, the more clearly and distinctly the answer seems to come. I call it 'surrendering to the universe', and it seems almost miraculous sometimes.

Admittedly, 'the universe' may bring an unexpected answer, and the route to the solution may be a bit winding, but later, on reflection, there's usually a good reason for that.

When you've had a bit of practice at identifying some of the feelings that are troubling your mind, and hopefully begun to experience what it feels like to be free from them, even for the briefest moment, which is the way it usually happens to start with, make the most of that free feeling by doing the next breathing exercise.

Breathing Exercise 10

'Breathing in, I make my mind happy. Breathing out, I make my mind happy.'

I hope that through your practice and self-awareness, you are beginning to find more inner peace, at least for short periods. When you do the following breathing exercise, see if you can allow the breath to take you to that peaceful part of yourself, so you can enjoy the feeling, and gladden your mind...

Take a mindfulness breath; simply notice the feeling of peace you can feel when the wanting, anger, or indecision is gone.

Say, 'Breathing in, I make my mind happy. Breathing out, I make my mind happy.'

Feel the peace. Feel the joy that this brings. Enjoy this beautiful feeling.

Mindfulness meditation

When you have been practising mindfulness breathing for a while, and have been able to experience something of the peace and joy it brings, you may like to extend your practice a little, into a short period of meditation. People make a big thing about meditation, but really, the kind of meditation I am talking about, what the Buddha taught and practised, is only joined-up mindfulness breaths. You take a mindfulness breath in the way we have been doing throughout this book – and then you take another, and another: if you're a Buddhist monk you may continue doing this for periods of an hour or more, throughout the day, interspersed with a walking meditation (see page 54) from time to time.

When I say 'only' joined-up mindfulness, that may sound simple, but of course the mind tries to intervene, the body twitches or aches, a siren sounds… it takes practice and persistence. But it gets easier with practice and brings so many benefits. In research studies, 10 minutes of meditation daily was found to be noticeably beneficial; 20 minutes, even more so.[2] You could start with just a few minutes, and gently increase the time when you feel ready. I find fitting in two or three short meditations (of anything from 5 to 20 minutes each depending on the situation) during the day, along with the mindfulness breaths that I take anyway whenever I think about it, gives a nice background sense of peace – on a good day, that is!

Give it a try and find out what suits you:

- Find a quiet place where you won't be disturbed.
- Sit with your spine straight.
- Breathe mindfully...

That's it. 'Keep it simple' is the best advice and don't play music, which distracts the mind. As the monk said in *I Met A Monk*: 'If you're meditating, meditate. If you're listening to music, listen to music. That's being mindful.'

'Meditation is not work, it is play... meditation is not something to be done to achieve some goal – peace, bliss – but something to be enjoyed as an end in itself.'

OSHO

My experience: **Meditation 1**

For many years I believed meditation was 'a good thing to do', but I didn't enjoy it much. However, all that changed as I learnt mindfulness breathing. I started to love it; the feeling of inner strength, peace and joy that it brought me.

My experience: **Meditation 2**

This is what the Buddha said about preparing to do mindfulness meditation:

> 'Here is one gone to the forest or to the root of a tree or to an empty hut, sit down; having folded your legs crosswise, set your body erect, and established mindfulness in front of the face – at the tip of the nose – ever mindful you breathe in, mindful you breathe out.'

We needn't go to quite those lengths, but I must say I love the simplicity of those instructions, and the fact *that we can practise mindfulness meditation anywhere, free as air, with no need for any material things. Having said that, I must admit that my favourite place to meditate is sitting in the half-lotus position, bolt upright in bed supported by the headboard and pillows! A far cry from the Buddha's 'root of a tree', but it works for me.*

A sanctuary within

You will find that mindfulness breathing takes you inside yourself to a place of peace, a place that 'knows'. As you go to this place your path there will become more clear, your trust more sure, the peace and wisdom you receive more certain.

The more you practise being mindful of your breath, even for a few minutes at a time, the more aware you will become of the 'mindfulness you' and the stronger the connection will get.

That place within where your mindfulness breath takes you will begin to feel like a sanctuary or a haven. The Buddha described it as being like an island within, but it may feel like a still pool of golden light, or a cushion of air, gently lifting you over the bumps of life: you will discover for yourself how it feels for you.

Ajahn Chah, the wise Thai monk who brought Buddhism to the West in the 1970s, experienced this place within as a 'clear still pool', and said.

'Try to be mindful, and let things take their natural course. Then your mind will become still in any surroundings, like a clear forest pool. All kinds of wonderful, rare animals will come to drink at the pool, and you will clearly see the nature of all things. You will see many strange and wonderful things come and go, but you will be still. This is the happiness of the Buddha.'[7]

That is how it often seems to me, too, though sometimes it seems very translucent, a pool of pale golden light rather than of water, or maybe it's a mixture of the two. It is always still and peaceful, and fills me with joy. But for each of us it is our own unique experience: we each find our inner place of peace.

Feel your own inner sense of peace and strength as you concentrate on your breath, and allow it to take you within yourself. Feel and sense, rather than picture anything. Open yourself to the moment and over time the peace within you, at your centre, will build. It happens naturally, you'll see.

Breathing Exercise *11*

'*Breathing in, I concentrate my mind. Breathing out, I concentrate my mind.*'

Take a mindfulness breath, and simply notice the feeling of peace that is there when the wanting, anger, or indecision is gone...

Feel the peace. Feel the joy that this brings. Enjoy this beautiful feeling.

As you breathe mindfully your breath soothes you. It distances you from the thoughts or feelings that are troubling you.

Breathe in; breathe out; notice and feel your breathing.

Feel the breath taking you into yourself; feel the peace there, if only for a moment.

You are safe; this is your place of security and peace. The more you breathe mindfully, the more you will connect with this place within, and the more you will value it and feel the peace, the strength, the clarity and wisdom that it holds

You will realize it is the deepest part of you; the part that holds your natural wisdom, the part that is kind and forgiving; the part that, when you connect with it, feels strong, free, peaceful and happy.

A simple code for happiness

As you continue with your mindfulness breathing and experience the peace this brings, you may find yourself naturally wanting to bring your outer life in line with your inner life.

Living a way of life that supports the breathing and the inner peace that you are touching really helps the whole process. That is why the Buddha gave his followers a simple code of behaviour called the 'Five Precepts'. These are five guidelines for living in a way that leads to a lifestyle that supports mindfulness and brings inner peace and happiness for everyone.

We can help ourselves in the process of mindfulness by living in such a way; the five precepts are:
1. Not killing
2. Not lying
3. Not stealing
4. Not misusing sex
5. Not abusing intoxicants.

There's nothing judgemental about this, it's just practical. For further guidance, the Buddha did define 'stealing' as 'taking that which is not given'.

Regarding sex, the Buddha did not condemn homosexuality in particular. He clarified that 'misuse of sex' means having sex with 'those under the protection of their father, mother, brother, sister, relatives or clan; or of their religious community; or with those promised to someone else, protected by law and even with those betrothed'.

Simple rule of life: treat all living beings (animals as well as people) as you would like to be treated; fairly, honestly, with consideration, kindness and respect.

Freedom

As we become increasingly mindful, we start living more 'in the now', accepting things as they are, whilst also realizing that they are changing all the time. So we learn to accept life 'as it is', and experience the increasing harmony, peace and happiness this brings. As you continue with your mindfulness practice you will begin to experience this for yourself. Enjoy that sense of freedom with the final breathing exercise in this section:

Breathing Exercise 12

'Breathing in, I liberate my mind. Breathing out, I liberate my mind.'

This is a breath of freedom, for now you understand about 'the three poisons' – greed, hate and delusion (see page 120) – and how they can affect your mind and cause suffering for you and other people, you know that you have a choice.

You don't have to let emotions and thoughts knock you around... you can liberate yourself...

As you breathe in, say to yourself, 'Breathing in, I liberate my mind.'

As you breathe out, say to yourself, 'Breathing out, I liberate my mind.'

Keep taking gentle mindfulness breaths...

Allow them to take you to that still, pure, mindfulness space within you.

Here you can just watch your emotions as if from afar – or even, eventually, you won't even notice them – or maybe they will just be little ripples on your inner pool as they simply subside, and you remain in peace.

You are free.

The authentic you

Mindfulness puts you in touch with a deeper, more 'authentic' part of you, and with your own unique inner power, the power that knows what is right for you; guides you and looks after you.

The more you practise mindfulness breathing and meditation, the more you will experience this power working in your life, and the more confidence you will have in it.

Little things fall into place, you are protected from harm, you meet the right people at the right moment, and the more you realize this is happening, the more you will let go the need to control, because you realize you can.

This surrender in turn increases the flow of support and guidance you get. It seems almost magical; it is certainly transformative.

Being in the flow

When we resist things in life, instead of going with the stream, it's as if we bump against the rocks.

And when we cling to things – our possessions, our views, our beliefs, our plans – it's as though we're hanging on to the reeds instead of going with the tide.

I like to think of my spirit as a clear mountain stream, and I try to keep the water clean and pure by living according to the five precepts, not allowing the 'three poisons' – greed, hatred and delusion – to pollute the water; to trust life and not cling to the reeds or bump up against the rocks, but to go with the flow of life, knowing it is taking care of me.

Surrender to this moment now

Surrender to this moment: when you breathe in, and out, and you give yourself to this moment and you feel at peace. You flow with the breath of life. Thoughts come and go like clouds in the sky passing by… when you think thoughts of attack, judgement or criticism, they bring a feeling of unease, they cloud the sky. Let them go. Breathe… be in this moment.

Mindfulness changes you from the inside out

It makes you kinder, more forgiving, more grateful, more honest, more tolerant, more joyful, freer, because it puts you in touch with the best of you, your inner awareness, your 'mindfulness centre' – the part of you that is all those things.

Being in touch with this part of you changes you. It changes the way you feel, think and behave, and when these things change in you, other people's attitude and behaviour to you change too, and so life changes.

The internal guidance system

We may find that we get more connected to our own inner source of wisdom; a kind of knowing, a sixth sense. We may find too that we are more trusting of the universe, and sense we are protected and guided in our life. Coincidences and synchronicities may happen more and more frequently that reinforce this belief.

Chapter 5

Free Your Spirit to Flow with Life

'All conditioned things are impermanent: when one sees this with wisdom, one turns away from suffering.'

THE BUDDHA

As we've practised being mindful we've become used to opening our awareness to 'what is', and accepting life as it is in this moment. In doing so, we've noticed things change, even as we're observing them – and we've come to accept that, too.

If a petal falls from a rose as we watch it, or a dark cloud passes over the sun and the rain begins to fall, a dog barks, or a siren sounds, well, so be it: that's the way things are.

So in our mindfulness we have naturally experienced the inevitability of change and learnt to accept and embrace it, letting things be, letting them flow, as we remain 'in the moment'.

In fact we've been observing for ourselves one of the cornerstones of the Buddha's teaching: 'the law of impermanence' – that everything that is created is subject to change.

Accepting this is a big step toward finding inner peace: being in the present moment whilst accepting the inevitability of change – that's the key.

Freedom from suffering

When still a teenager the Buddha – who was called Siddhartha Gautama – knew that his life's work would be to find the reason for suffering and how it could be ended. That was why he spent several years wandering in the wilderness and fasting; and why, having failed in his search, he sat down under a fig tree (later called a Bodhi tree due to Siddhartha's enlightenment there), breathed mindfully, and vowed he would stay there until he had found the answer.

All night long he sat, as the full moon traversed the sky. Then, as the moon set in the west, and the first rays of sunlight warmed his face, he opened his eyes.

He had found the answer; and it was this:

· Everything that is created is impermanent.
· Therefore becoming attached to anything causes suffering.

- The way out of suffering is through being mindful of the present moment and living in a way that does not create attachments.

Thus 'Buddhism' was born, although the Buddha never called it that; the name evolved from the Sanskrit verb *budh*, meaning 'awaken', which is what the teaching is all about, and something that every human being can do.

So, it is in accepting that everything changes – impermanence – and thus learning not to depend on anything for our happiness and peace of mind, or allowing anything to disturb us – being 'non-attached' - that we find true peace and happiness.

So let's allow ourselves a few minutes of quietude and peace to be mindful of our breathing, as we practise the next breathing exercise and allow the thought of impermanence to rest in our mind, seeing if we can experience the timeless peace this brings.

Being truly mindful helps us
whatever we are going through;
this breath, now, is all there is,
and all is well in this moment,
so we can be at peace.

Breathing Exercise 13

'Breathing in, I observe the impermanence of life.
Breathing out, I observe the impermanence of life.'

Breathing, say to yourself, 'I observe impermanence. Breathing out, I observe impermanence...'

Breathing in, 'I follow the breath and allow it to take me into a place of peace within.'

Breathing out, 'I am aware of the impermanence of the breath.'

Breathing in, 'I rest in my centre of peace as one breath ends...'

Breathing out, 'I wait; I feel the next breath gently form...'

Breathing in, 'I am aware of the rising and falling of my chest...'

Breathing out, 'The impermanence of my breath...'

Breathing in, 'The peace I am experiencing.'

Enjoy the peace and strength of several breaths

– or for several minutes, depending on what feels right for you, then allow yourself a few moments to come back to everyday awareness, and gently open your eyes

When you're happy, allow yourself to appreciate the moment, knowing it will pass; and when you're sad or worried, when things are difficult – desperate even – remember this: this too will pass.

My experience: **The law of impermanence**

I find knowing about and accepting the law of impermanence helpful, particularly when I'm going through a difficult time: it stands to reason that if change is inevitable, the bad times will pass, the sadness and the worry will end. And knowing this helps me to find peace in the present moment. You can tell I am a 'glass half full' kind of person, because of course 'impermanence' applies to the ending of the good times, too. But I tell myself that's all the more reason for being 'in the now' and really appreciating them while they last.

Accepting change

Any reasonable person can accept that change is a part of life, but coping with it is another matter!

The secret is to be able to appreciate things fully in this present moment, so that we flow with life and accept 'what is', whilst knowing that change will come, and that when it does, we can take that, too, in our stride.

This is a great art to have, and the key to it lies in one word, which – along with impermanence – is another cornerstone of the Buddha's teaching: 'non-attachment'. In fact, understanding and practising 'non-attachment' could change your life because it's being attached to things that causes us pain.

So what does 'non-attachment' mean? What, indeed, are 'attachments?'

Well, let me ask you a question, and then it might

become clearer. It starts with a story about the Buddha: bear with me!

How many cows have you got?

One day the Buddha was sitting having a picnic with a group of his monks when a distraught farmer came rushing by. The farmer asked whether they had seen his cows because they had all disappeared and he said he was the unhappiest man in the world; he was so upset he might kill himself.

The Buddha replied that they had not seen them; the cows must have gone in the opposite direction.

The farmer ran off and the Buddha observed to his monks that they must be the happiest men in the world because they didn't have any cows to lose.

'At first,' he said — or so the story goes — 'it might seem that those cows are essential to your happiness; you might even try to get more and more, but then you realize that the more you own, the more you have to *lose. That is why to be happy you have to learn the art of "cow-releasing".'*

I like that story because it's a reminder of the pain we feel when we lose something that we've become attached to.

And one of the most helpful things we can do for our happiness and peace of mind is to release our cows!

In other words, become aware of all the things in our life that we are attached to – and gently let go our attachment to them. And I have to say, when you start doing this, I think you will be amazed firstly at how many cows you own – and secondly, how wonderful it feels when you let them go!

Actually, the very action of noticing them, becoming aware of them, helps the releasing process, and it does get easier the more you release.

How many cows can you release?

You might not be able to spot your attachments at first. 'Attached? Me? I'm not attached to anything,' you might say. But the more you think about them, the more you'll find. And that's OK. It's OK to have attachments – we all do – but the great secret is *to be aware* of them.

Once you know they're there, their power over you lessens. They may still be there, but they're not pushing and shoving you around so much, compelling you to act, making you do things or say things that really, deep down, or, in retrospect, feel wrong to you – wrong to the mindfulness part of you.

And as you breathe and practise, this wise and peaceful mindfulness part of you is becoming stronger. You are beginning to be more and more aware of it. It will help you find your cows, shine a light on all the dark places they may be hiding, so you really can let them go, and as each one fades away, your sense of inner freedom and peace and joy will increase – as will your energy. It takes a lot of hidden energy to keep those cows locked up, you know!

How to recognize an attachment

To recognize any attachments use either of the following quick rules of thumb to assess them:

- You're attached to something or someone when any strong emotion is present: If the thought of either having it, or not having it arouses in you strong feelings, possibly anger, jealousy, hate, greed or lust, you can be sure that there is an attachment.
- You're attached to some idea or concept if there's 'should', or an 'ought' involved: What we think we should do, or others should do, the way things should be, the way the world ought to be run... There's always an attachment lurking when the words 'should' or 'ought' crop up – that's why they're words I do not generally use. If I begin to feel the need to use them, I feel my 'attachment warning bells' ringing and I look to see what is driving me...

There's no end to our attachments, really, and even when we've done a bit of work on ourselves and experienced some freedom from them, there's always a surprise one that will pop up and bite you when you're least expecting it. It may be to do with what seems like a really trifling little thing, like the other day when I lost my favourite pen. It was only an inexpensive one but I really loved the feel and the flow of it; it was an eye-opener to me how upset I felt, but a good reminder of letting go of attachments! (And I did find it eventually.)

The great thing is that once we have become aware of our attachments it means they no longer have hidden power over us; we – or rather our mindfulness self – is in control. And life becomes happier and more peaceful.

What are your attachments?

We can get attached to anything: people, our loved ones, possessions, places, where we live, where we like to go; money, possessions, fame, and success, a particular lifestyle, having money – or even not having money, if we think money is a bad thing – our work, the 'persona' we adopt for work.

Habits, things we always like to do, such buying a particular newspaper and reading it at a particular coffee shop, at a particular time; the place we stand on the

Suffering is caused by 'attachment to desire'; wanting something, not wanting it, wanting something different.

Life constantly changes; so if we become attached to anything, we suffer.

Letting go of desire is like anything else. It gets easier with practice. You'll know you've released your desire when you accept the situation exactly as it is.

platform waiting for the train to work in the morning and the seat we sit in...

Our philosophy, our long-held views and beliefs, our religion – if we've got one, or our lack on one if we haven't – rites and rituals.

The view we have of ourselves in the 'do you realize WHO I AM?' sense – such as pride in our family, our lineage, our roots, our nationality and so on, all this is called 'personality view', and we can let that go, too. This is not the real us, who we are deep down, it's just the persona we're inhabiting for this brief life.

We can be attached to what other people think of us, too: the 'clever one', the 'arty one', even sadly, 'the failure', 'the naughty one': descriptive tags that have nothing to do with who we really are inside, and need to be dropped.

My experience: **Attachments**

I don't like crowds and lining up; I'll go out of my way to avoid them, even getting somewhere really early to do so, which probably means I actually waste time in the long run. Also I really hate being late, or when other people are late. You see, I am saying 'hate' – a sure sign of the presence of some form of attachment. Like most people, I am also attached to certain possessions, such as the pen I mentioned before. And conditions: having light, tidiness, peace and quiet in my home – and silence, except of course when I am the one putting on the radio or the music! I'm very attached to living in a way that doesn't cause suffering to any living creatures, too: to me, that's a 'good thing', but it's still an attachment, and I am aware of that.

Letting go of attachments

Attachment is not necessarily 'bad' in itself – it's when you're not aware of it that problems arise. Recognizing the presence of an attachment is the main thing.

Ask yourself, are your attachments running the show? Who is master of your ship? Is it you, or is it some pesky little attachment that's pushing you around and spoiling things for you?'

Once we begin to notice the grip an attachment has on us, we can begin to let it go. That does not mean that we no longer care; that we become cold and closed off from our feelings.

It means that through our mindfulness we become aware of who or what arouses strong feelings in us – and once we're mindful of it, we put ourselves in the driving seat, and those feelings no longer have free rein.

We may still feel them, and, hey, we may still buy that newspaper and go to that coffee shop and sit in the corner seat by the window every day – but at least we're doing it whilst smiling at our 'attachment self', not being driven by it...

But now we know about it, when we feel a strong emotion arising, we can pause for a moment before speaking or acting. We can deal with the feeling behind the attachment in exactly the same way as we have learnt to do with all our feelings:

- **Observe** the feeling; perhaps identify it as being greed, hate or delusion, as we have already learnt to do, although we don't necessarily have to put a name on it;
- **Feel** the feeling; allow it to be, give it space inside you; and

• **Let the feeling go** – which it will do, of its own accord, just as any feeling does when given the 'observe/feel/let go' process.

So, one by one, you can let your attachments go; and every time one goes you'll feel that bit lighter and freer – without getting 'attached' to the process, of course... let it flow, let life flow.

*Knowing you can always breathe
and go to that place of peace
and strength within helps in the
loosening of attachments.*

The following breathing exercise is helpful, too.

Breathing Exercise *14*

'Breathing in, I observe the disappearance of desire.
Breathing out, I observe the disappearance of desire.'

Breathe in; notice how you are feeling; any tension in your jaw, your neck, your shoulders, your back, your body...

Be aware of the 'pull' or the desire of the attachment.

We are not trying to change things; we are accepting what we are feeling, allowing it to be there.

Take a few mindfulness breaths as you let the tension go...

Breathe in; feel the gentle breath healing you, as you breathe in, and out...

Breathing, say to yourself, 'I observe fading away of desire; breathing out, I observe fading away of desire...'

Continue gently following your breath, flowing with it, letting it be, feeling the tension fading.

Breathing in: 'I observe fading away of desire, breathing out, I observe fading away of desire...'
Breathing out: of the ties and bonds that are holding you in their grip...
Breathing out: letting them go, melting away...
Peace, and freedom are only a mindfulness breath away...

'The Buddha is like a full moon sailing across an empty sky; free, because he had no possessions, no attachments.'

BUDDHIST POEM, ANON.

Accepting 'what is'

'I want it like this, not like that,' we say; or 'I do want this, I don't want that.' When we think or say these things, we are fighting against 'what is'. We are doing what Ajahn Sumedho, whose writings I find so helpful, calls 'picking and choosing'.

How would it feel if instead of 'picking and choosing', pushing against it, you accept 'what is', say, 'It is as it is,' and feel the 'pull' of attachment go.

Feel the relaxation of the tension, the peace that brings.

It may be possible to change things in the future – they certainly *will* change, because everything changes, as we know. That can be 'good' if you want change, or 'bad' if you are clinging to things as they are. But change is inevitable in any case

When we can accept things as they are now, but recognize that they will change, and accept that too, we will know peace.

Breathe in; breathe out. Feel the peace and security of this moment now. All is well in this moment.

The way to peace

Whatever is happening around you, just be… breathe, and be in your mindfulness place of peace within, just 'being'; observing, at ease and accepting everything. Mindfulness is not judgemental, not condemning, not criticizing, not about picking and choosing, liking or disliking, trying to get something, or to get rid of something.

Mindfulness, this sense of awareness within, is totally accepting of everything: the pleasure or the pain in the body, the good thoughts or the bad thoughts; the happiness or the sadness, despair, or whatever emotional quality you are experiencing.

Feel the peace of this moment now,
as we practise the next breathing
exercise: the cessation of suffering,
as we become free from attachments.

Breathing Exercise 15

'*Breathing in, I observe cessation. Breathing out,
I observe cessation.*'

Take a few mindfulness breaths to bring you to
that place of peace and purity within.

Open yourself to what is there for you; it may feel
like pure, transparent space...

As though you are on a mountaintop with the
open clear sky above, or 'vast emptiness'.

Empty, free, open and eternal, vibrant with life...

Breathe...

Your mind and heart empty but full, still but alive,
alone but at one with all.

Breathe... and return to your everyday consciousness.

I like the feeling of utter peace and purity that the word 'cessation' brings. And the more you meditate on it, the more life you find in that peace and purity within. You will begin to understand what the Bodhidharma, the Buddhist teacher who brought Zen Buddhism to China, in the sixth century, meant when he spoke of 'vast emptiness'... such an indescribably beautiful, expansive, clear, feeling: beyond words.

'Your mind is nirvana.'

BODIDHARMA

Breathing Exercise 16

'*Breathing in, I observe letting go. Breathing out, I observe letting go.*'

As you might expect, this final breathing exercise follows on from the last one when we experienced the absolute peace and purity of cessation, like the stillness at the centre of the wheel, where the power is stored, connected to the whole by every spoke. It is really beyond words; you will experience it for yourself. There is no thinking, no 'doing' involved, just being and letting go. It will happen.

No words, just being;

Free from attachment, pure and clear;

Resting in the perfect peace of now;

At one with all.

WE ARE ALL ONE.

The stream of life

The same stream of life that runs
  through my veins night and day
   runs through the world and dances
  in rhythmic measures.

It is the same life that shoots in joy
  through the dust of the earth in
  numberless blades of grass and
  breaks into tumultuous waves
  of leaves and flowers.

It is the same life that is rocked in the
  ocean-cradle of birth and of death,
  in ebb and in flow.

RABRINDRANATH TAGORE

Epilogue

Whilst I was writing this book I experienced the death of my beloved husband, Robert, to whom I had been married for over 50 years. It was not unexpected; as readers of my previous book, I Met A Monk, will know, he had been taken ill, very suddenly, with Lewy Body Dementia. When I wrote that book, I was still nursing him at home, but within a few months the deterioration in his condition meant that he had to go first to our local hospital, where he was treated for several months, and then to a high-dependency nursing home.

I visited him at both places daily for over 15 months, watching helplessly as he rapidly deteriorated in mind and body. I was sustained by the unbelievably selfless care and kindness he (and I) received. I was blessed that even when he could no longer speak, he did still recognize me. Almost until his last day his eyes would light up when he saw me, and the final thing he did before he drifted peacefully away in his sleep was squeeze my hand. I am truly thankful for that.

That was nearly four months ago now, and since then I have often felt his presence, and a strange thing has been happening. From time to time throughout the day both my hands suddenly become really hot. It makes me smile because I am certain it's a sign from Robert, in spirit, that he is close, because he always had warm hands and mine are always cold, and sometimes he used to hold my hands to warm them. When this happens it often seems as though he is reassuring me over some issue that is on my mind, and I am so thankful for that. And of course it links back to his time in the nursing home when all he could do to communicate with me was hold my hand, and that last hand squeeze just a few hours before he died. I also feel him close – my hands burning hot – when I am meditating. We used to meditate together sometimes when he was alive, so now, with my eyes shut, and aware of his presence, it feels comfortingly familiar.

That's not to say I don't experience much sadness. Some days every little thing keeps reminding me of him, it may be the presence of something – such as catching sight of one of his possessions – one of his tools in his untidy workroom, cast down from the last time he used it; his coat still on a peg by the back door, one of his treasured books or CDs, a straggly, unfinished scribbled note in wobbly handwriting, reminding me like a stab in the heart of when his illness began to take hold.

Or on the other hand, it can be the *lack* of something that sets me off: no sound of the lawnmower going, or of the cricket on the television; no sight of him, in his jeans and wellingtons, stripped to the waist, lean and tanned, not looking anywhere near his calendar age, trimming the tall hedge or cutting back a vigorous shrub. At first I found weekends particularly sad and difficult; I still do, if I'm honest; no long, leisurely breakfast with the newspapers, competing noisily over who can answer the crossword clues first, no happy discussion of plans for the day – often, no plans at all, actually: just empty hours ahead, and reminders all around me of happier times.

When you've been together for as long as we had, your lives are so woven together that memories lie everywhere. A snatch of music on the radio, an advertisement through the door for an opera we enjoyed together; the sight of a couple walking with their arms entwined, a sudden mention of a place visited, an activity enjoyed... these are like rubbing salt into a wound, yet I know the feelings of sadness and loss have to be experienced in order to be released, and that this process can't be hurried.

I have been so blessed that, apart from writing a few articles and working on this book, my time has been relatively free. My three daughters have all been incredible: so loving, supportive and helpful in every way – and they have encouraged me to accept things as they are, and to grieve, and that in itself has been so helpful. The many quiet days I have been able to spend at home – sometimes (often) just giving up on the day and going to bed – have been so healing, and gradually, very gradually, I am beginning to feel stronger and less like a constantly flowing stream of emotion.

The mindfulness breathing that I have described in this book has been well and truly tested by my situation, and it really has helped me. When I feel upset about the past, or worried about the future, or just plain sad, I breathe in, and gently bring myself back to the present, and the peace of 'this moment now'. I remind myself that memories are of the past, and fears are of the future, and that when I breathe mindfully, I can bring myself into the present and feel the peace – and the joy – of 'now'. And that is a great blessing and I feel I am beginning to emerge. In fact I sometimes I feel like a butterfly about to come out of its chrysalis, eyes unused to the light, wings still crumpled and damp, but ready to open up in the warm air, and fly... I hope my wings will be strong and brightly coloured, and that the sun will shine...

Notes on the Text

1. http://plumvillage.org/sutra/discourse-on-the-full-awareness-of-breathing/; accessed 20 May 2016
2. http://news.harvard.edu/gazette/story/2011/01/eight-weeks-to-a-better-brain/; accessed 18 May 2016
3. http://www.sciencemag.org/news/2010/11/daydreaming-downer; accessed 18 May 2016
4. http://www.hongkiat.com/blog/how-to-increase-happiness/; accessed 18 May 2016
5. http://www.mindful.org/5-science-backed-ways-to-boost-your-happiness/; accessed 18 May 2016
6. http://greatergood.berkeley.edu/article/item/5_ways_giving_is_good_for_you; accessed 20 May 2016
7. Ajahn Chah, *Still Forest Pool* (Quest Books, 1996), page vi
8. Thich Nhat Hanh, *The Path of Emancipation* (Parallax Press, 2000), page 21

Acknowledgements

My sincere thanks to all those who helped make this book possible:

My agent, Barbara Levy; my publisher Jo Lal at Watkins; my wonderful editor, Sandy Draper, and the brilliant art and production team: Francesca Corsini, Gail Jones, Uzma Taj, Slav Todorov and Steve Williamson.

WATKINS

Sharing Wisdom Since
1893

The story of Watkins dates back to 1893, when the scholar of esotericism John Watkins founded a bookshop, inspired by the lament of his friend and teacher Madame Blavatsky that there was nowhere in London to buy books on mysticism, occultism or metaphysics. That moment marked the birth of Watkins, soon to become the home of many of the leading lights of spiritual literature, including Carl Jung, Rudolf Steiner, Alice Bailey and Chögyam Trungpa.

Today, the passion at Watkins Publishing for vigorous questioning is still resolute. Our wide-ranging and stimulating list reflects the development of spiritual thinking and new science over the past 120 years. We remain at the cutting edge, committed to publishing books that change lives.

DISCOVER MORE . . .

Read our blog

Watch and listen to
our authors in action

Sign up to
our mailing list

JOIN IN THE CONVERSATION

WatkinsPublishing   @watkinswisdom

watkinsbooks   watkinswisdom   watkins-media

Our books celebrate conscious, passionate, wise and happy living.
Be part of the community by visiting

www.watkinspublishing.com